Sacred Flowers

Coloring Book for Adults

by Asma Zergui

http://www.asmazergui.com

ISBN-13:
978-1511711791

ISBN-10:
1511711795

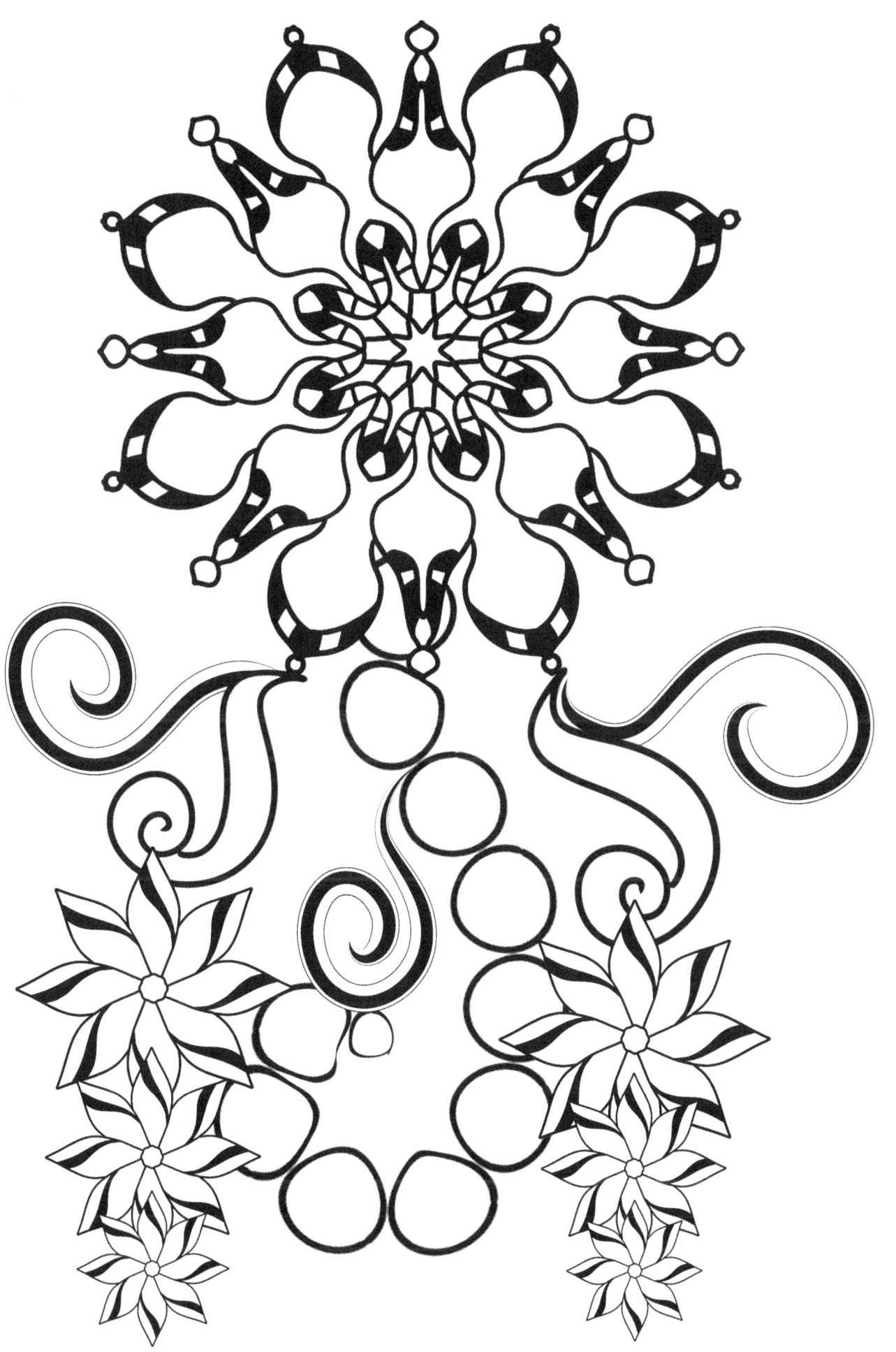

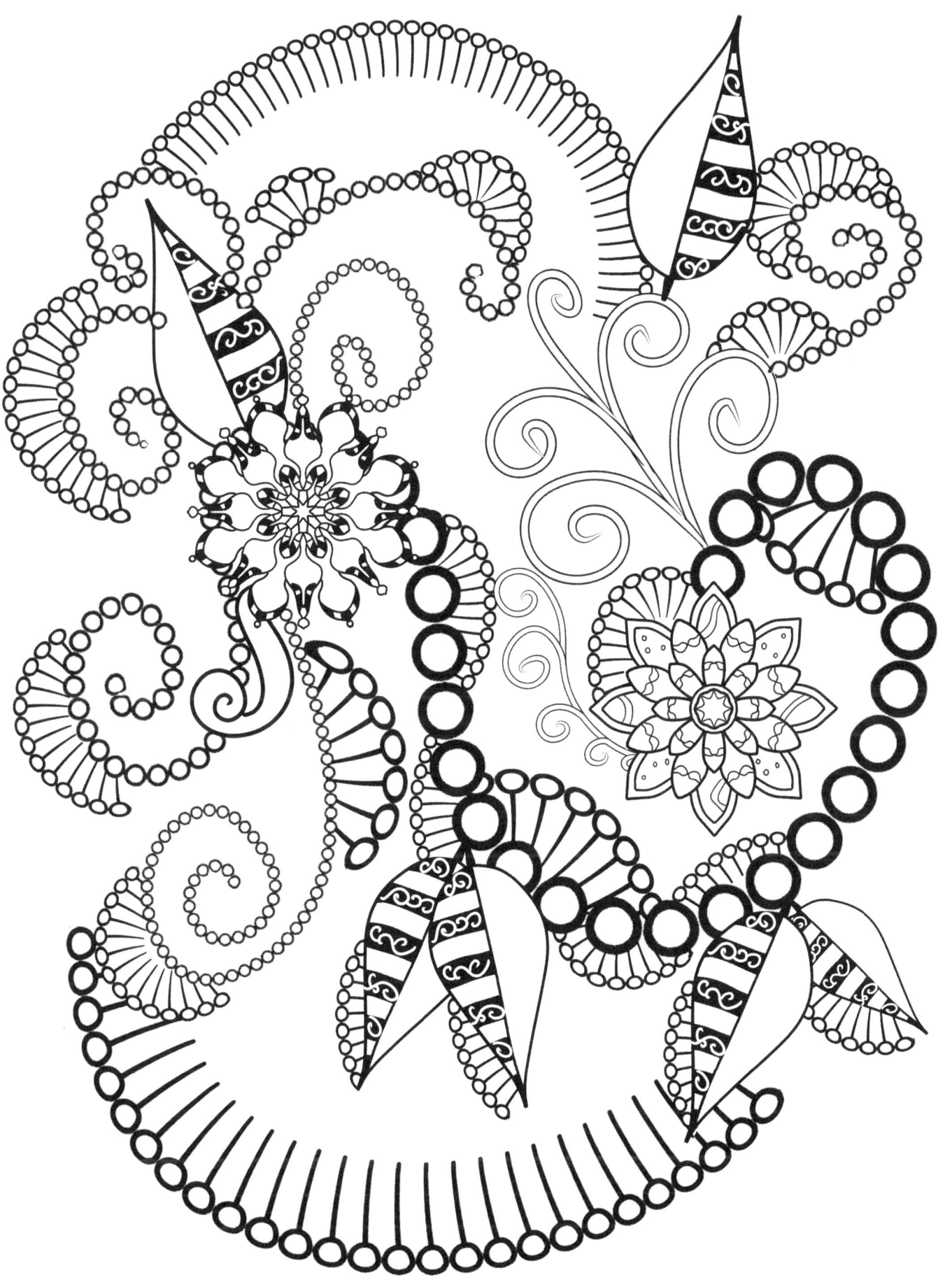

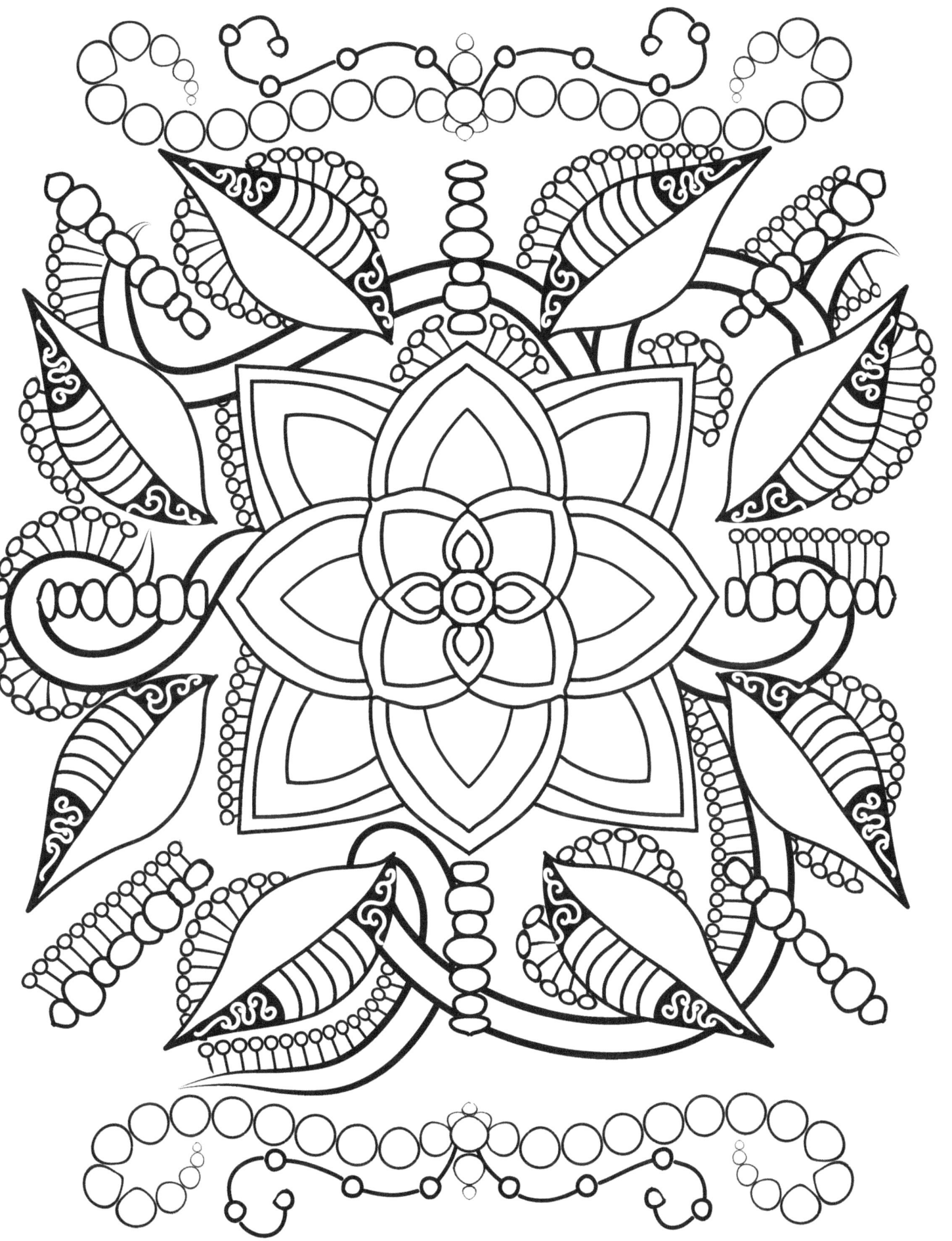

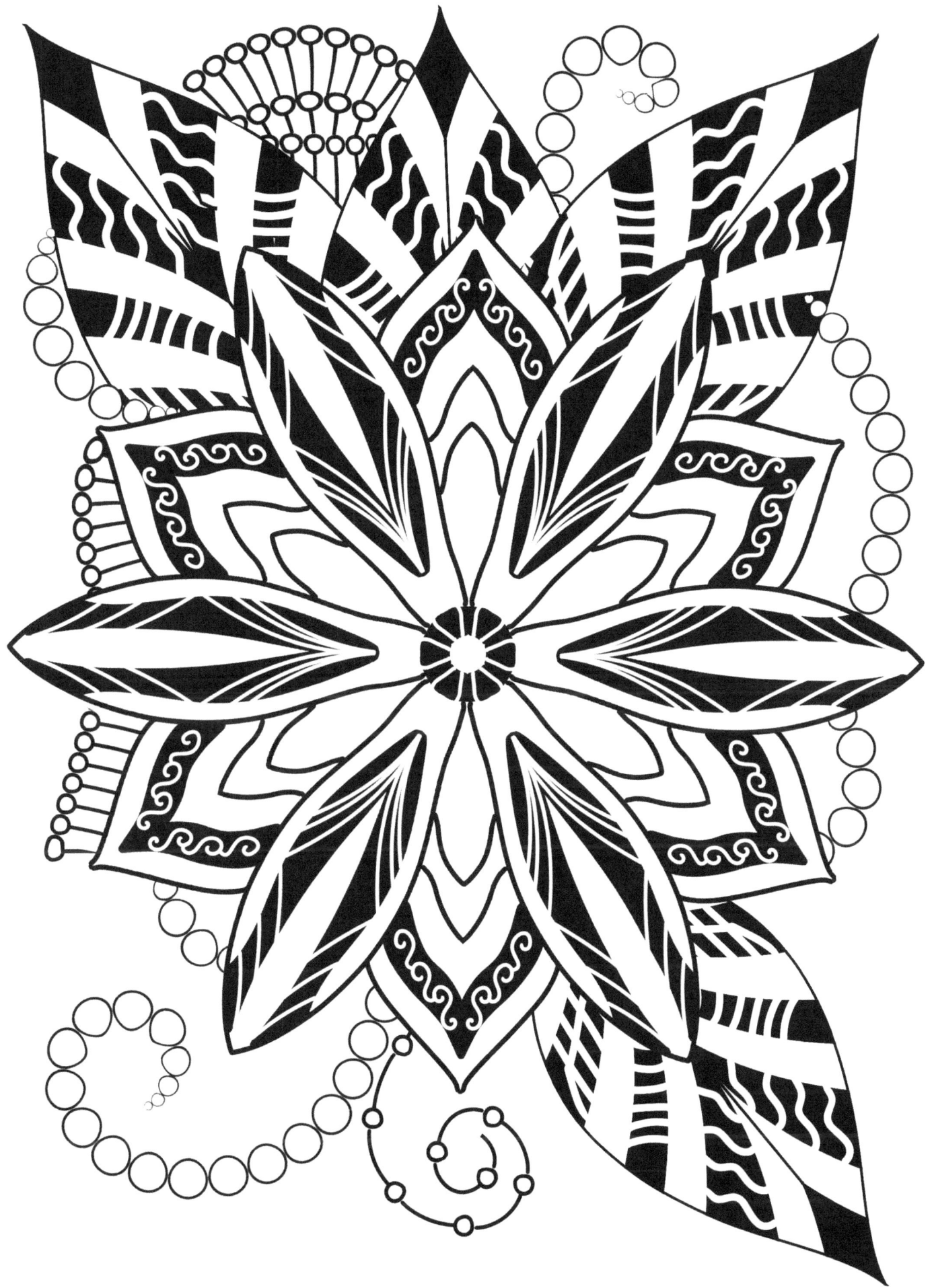

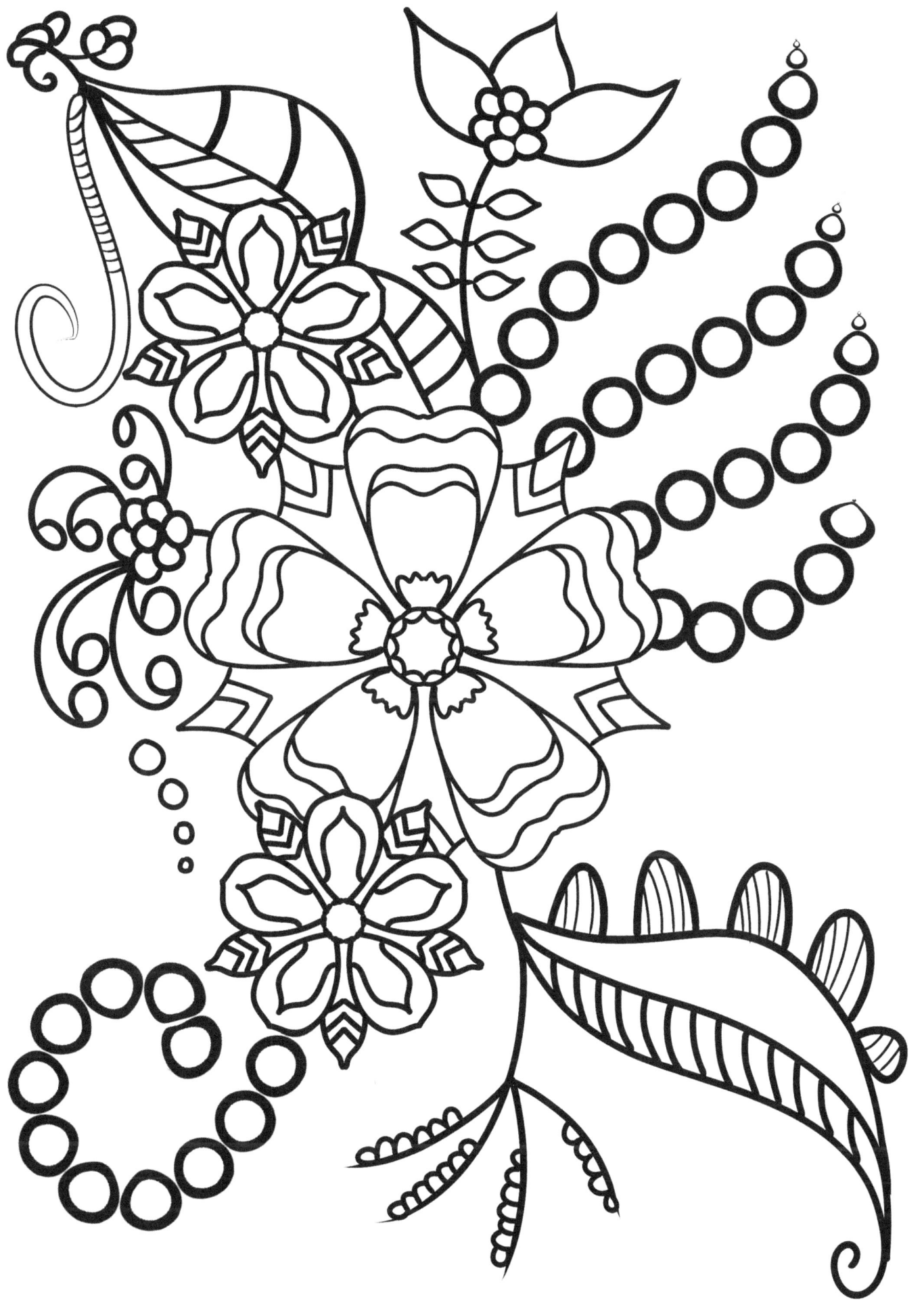

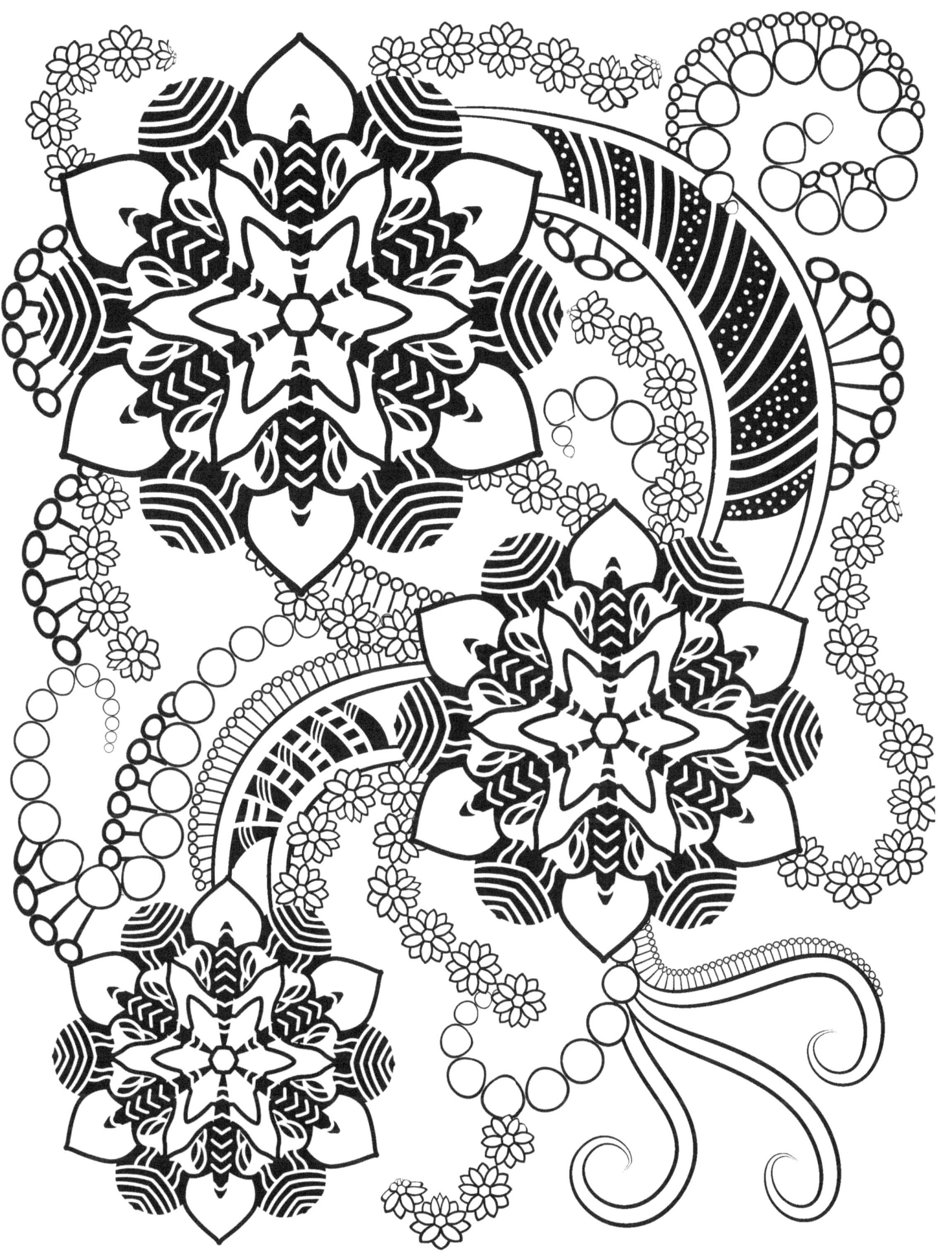

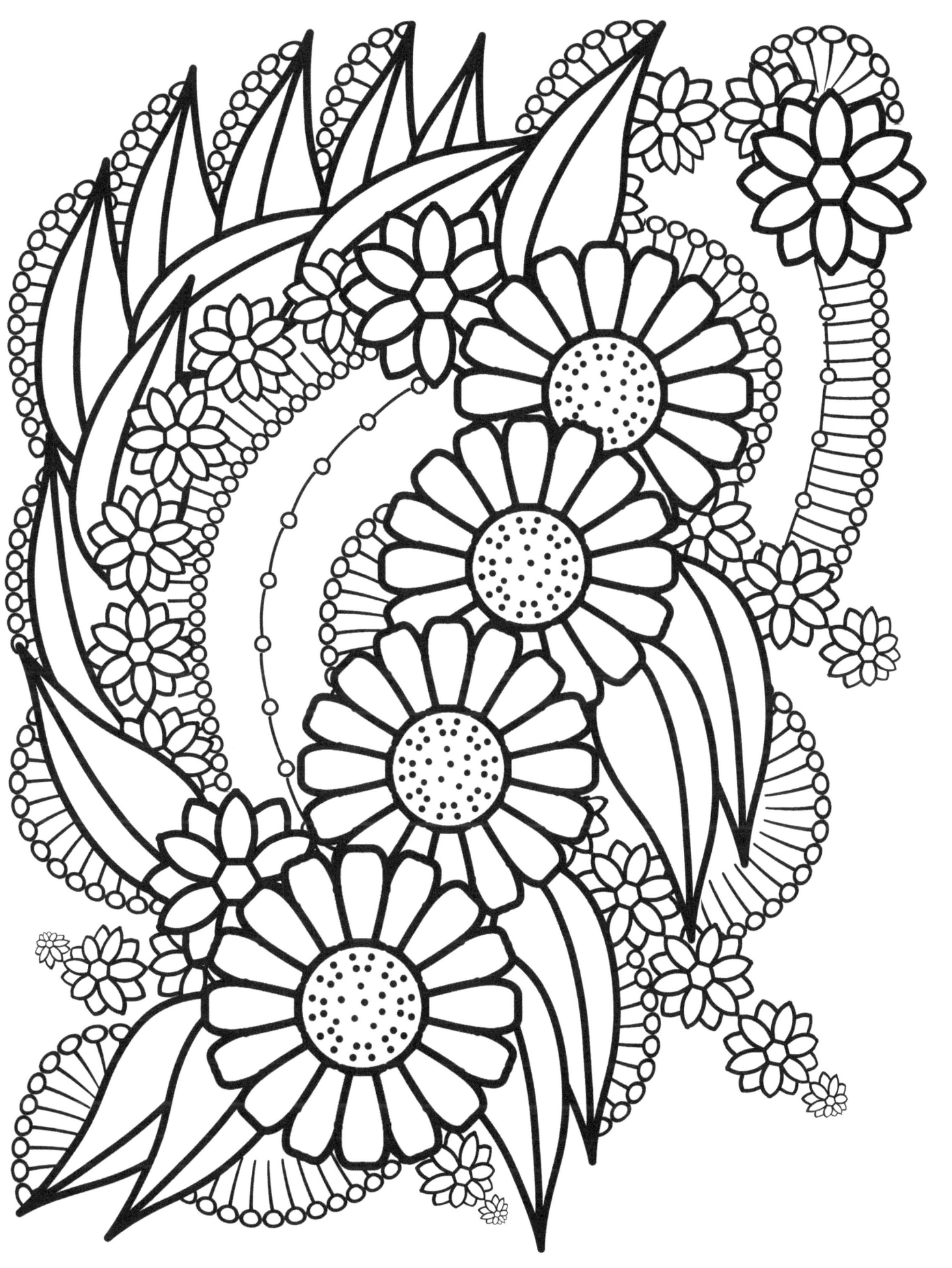

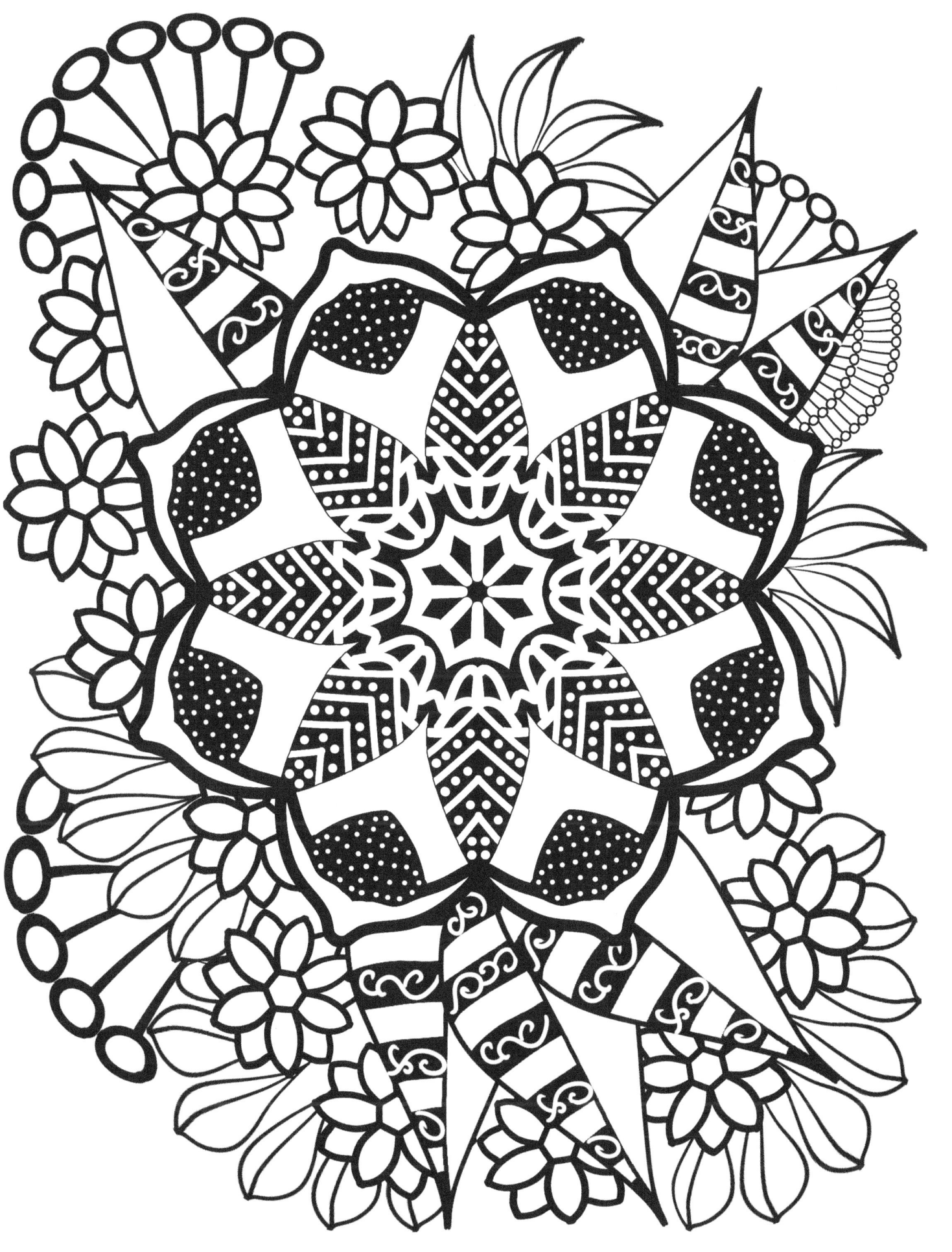

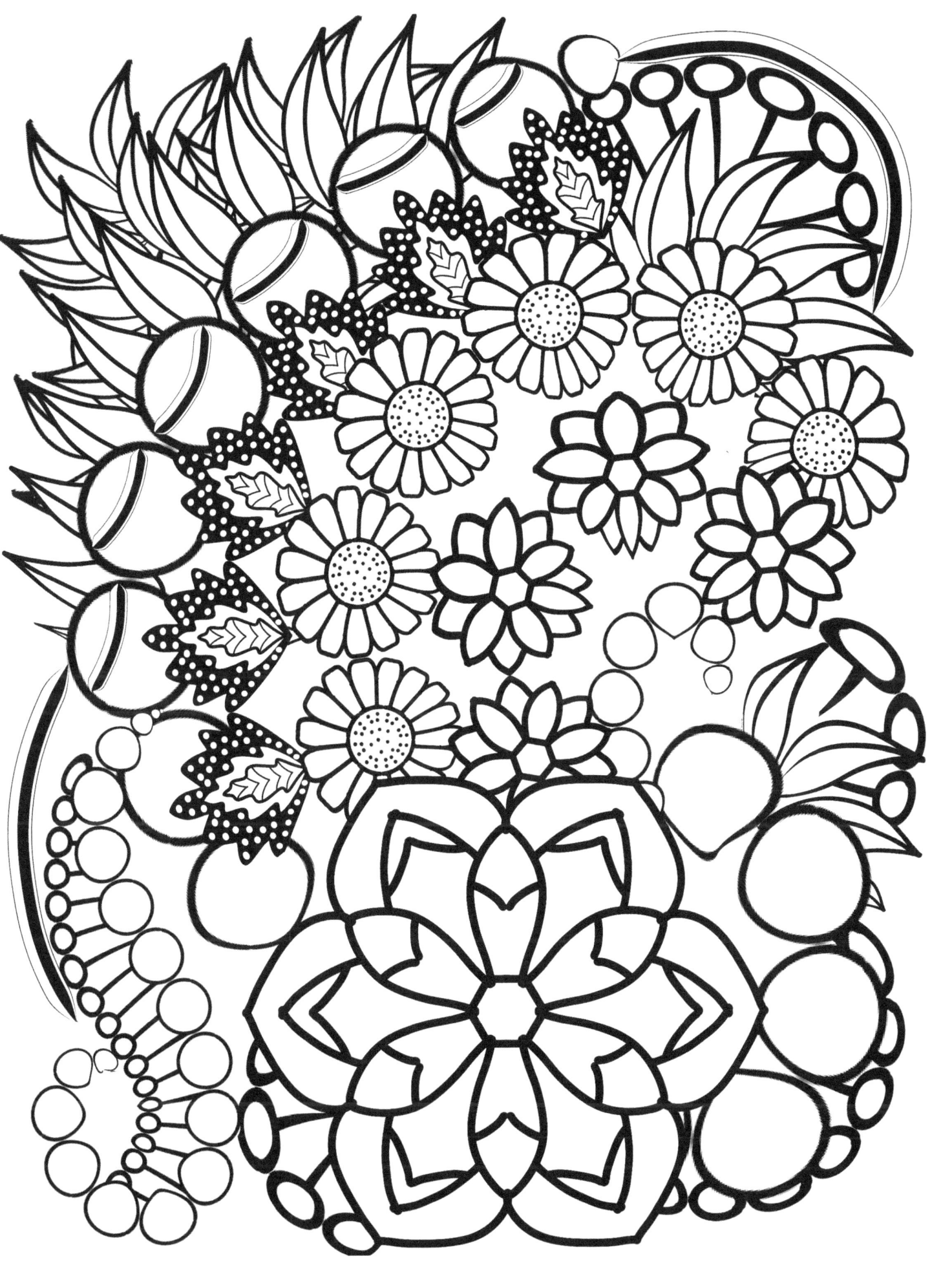

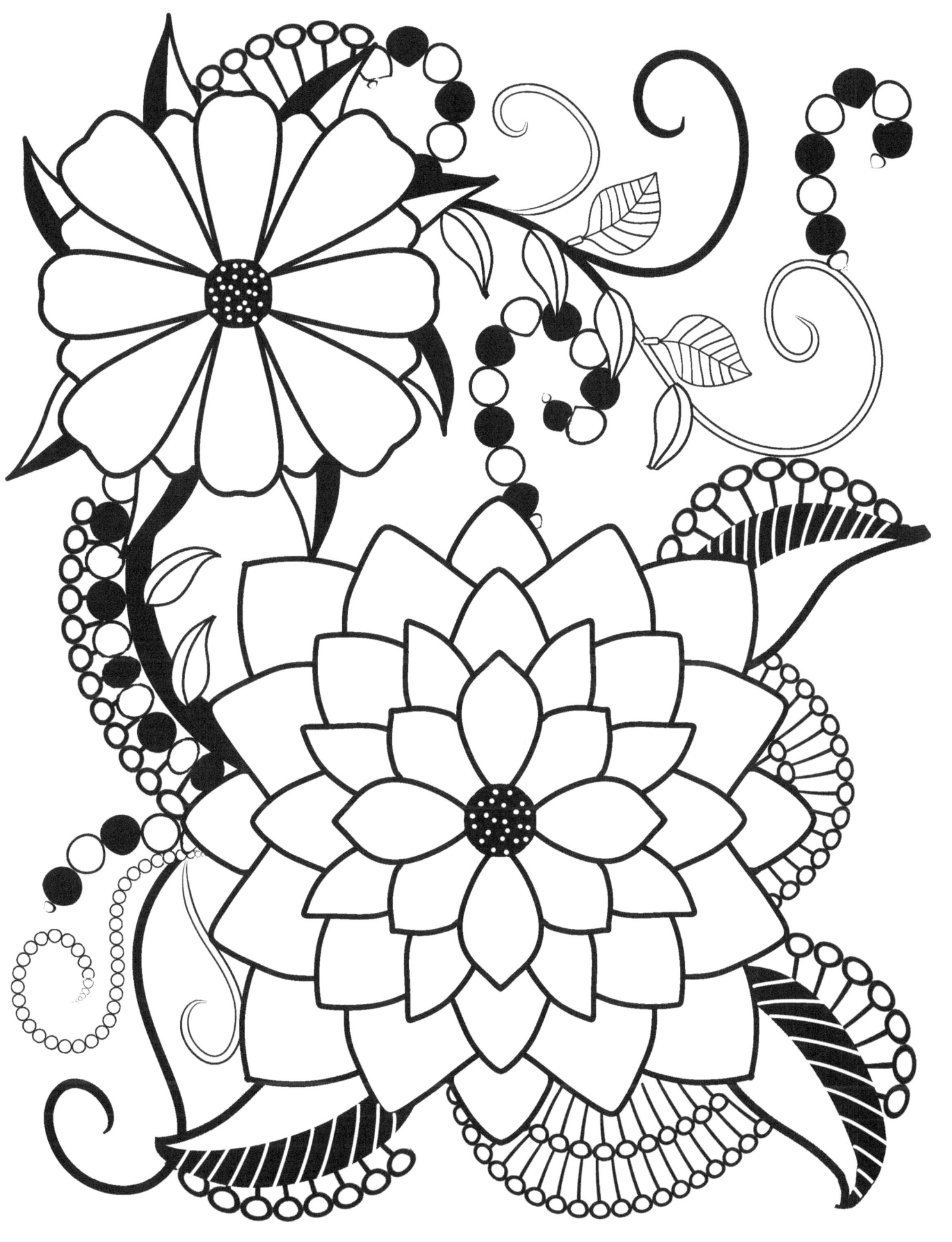

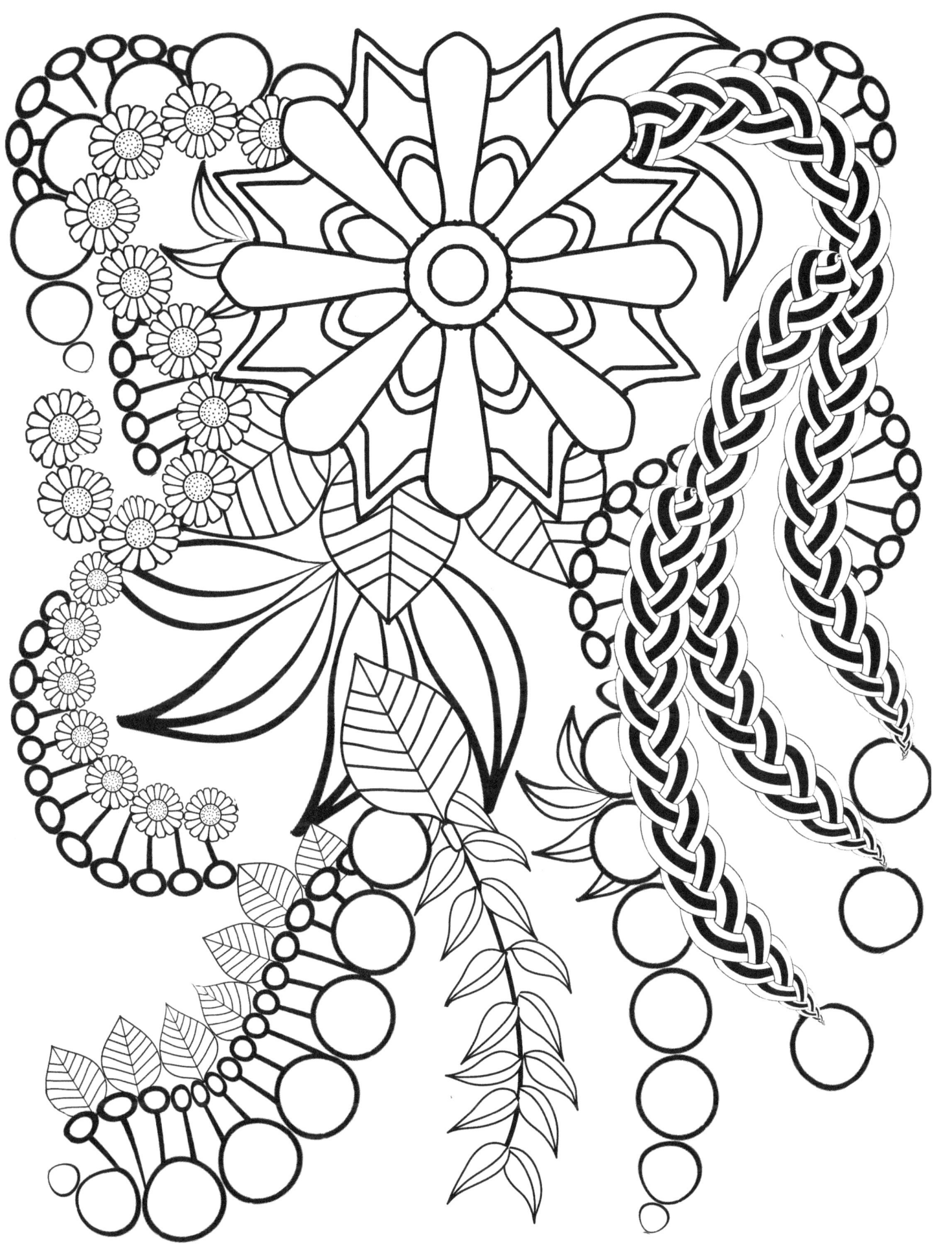

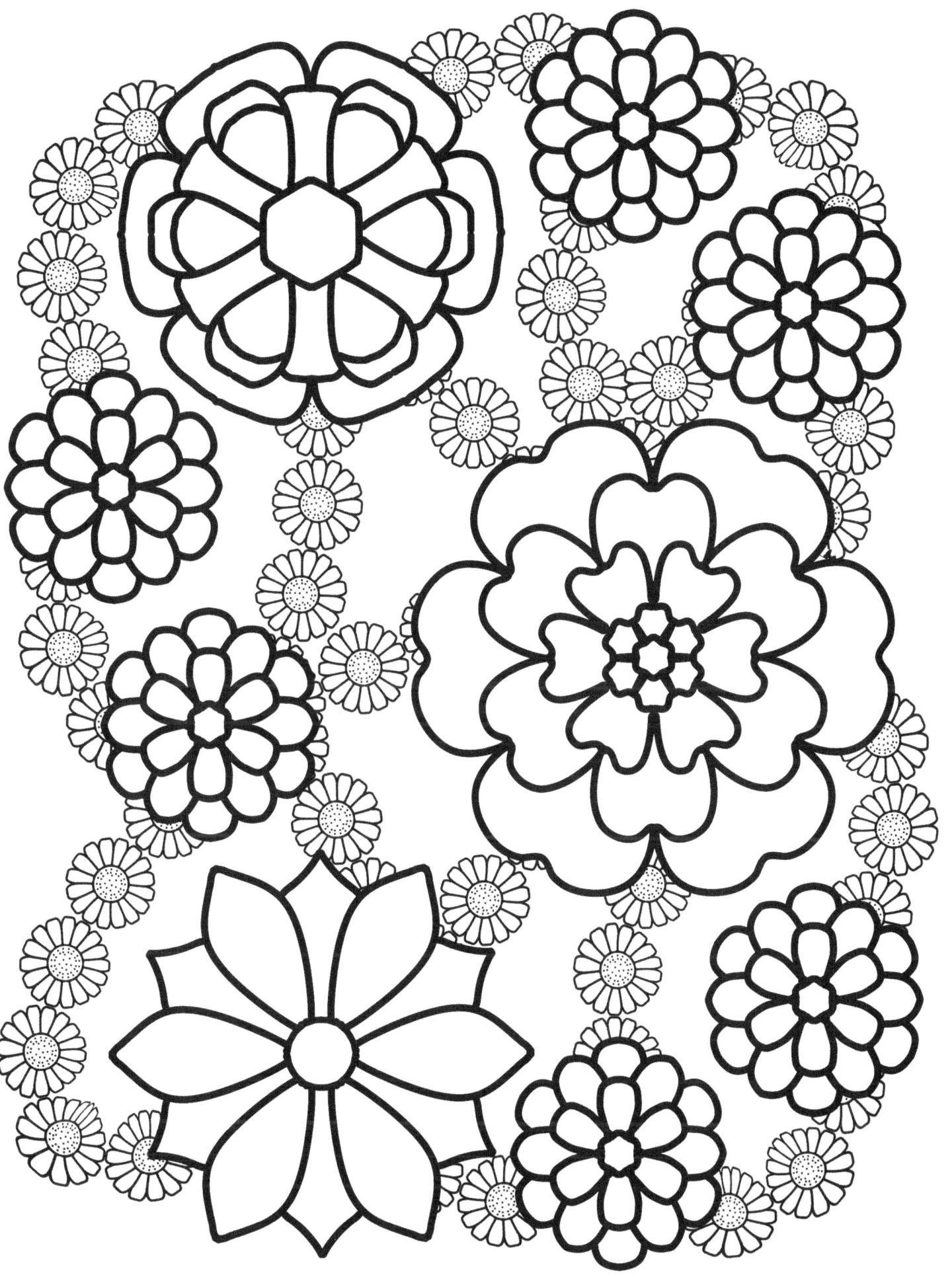

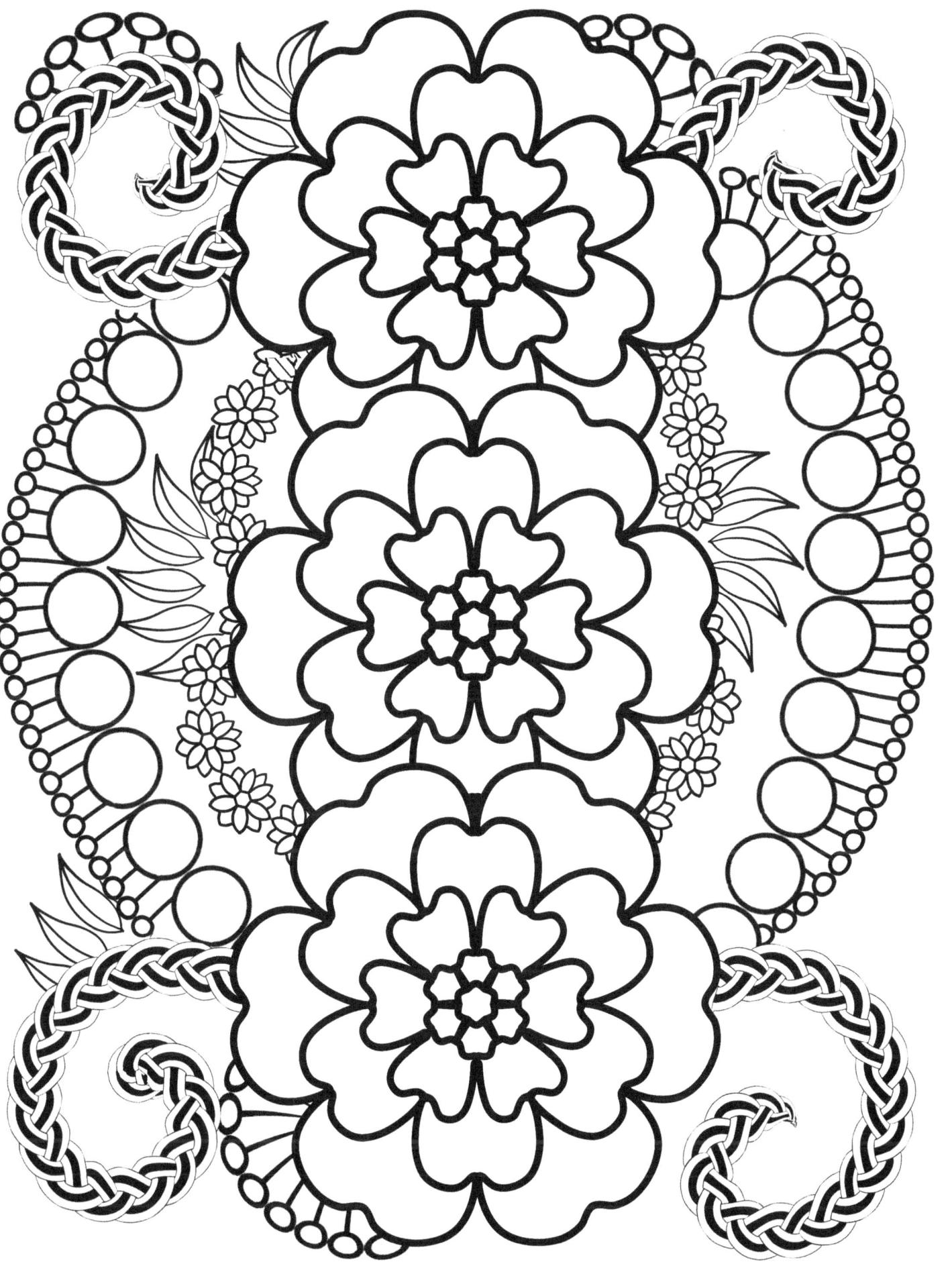

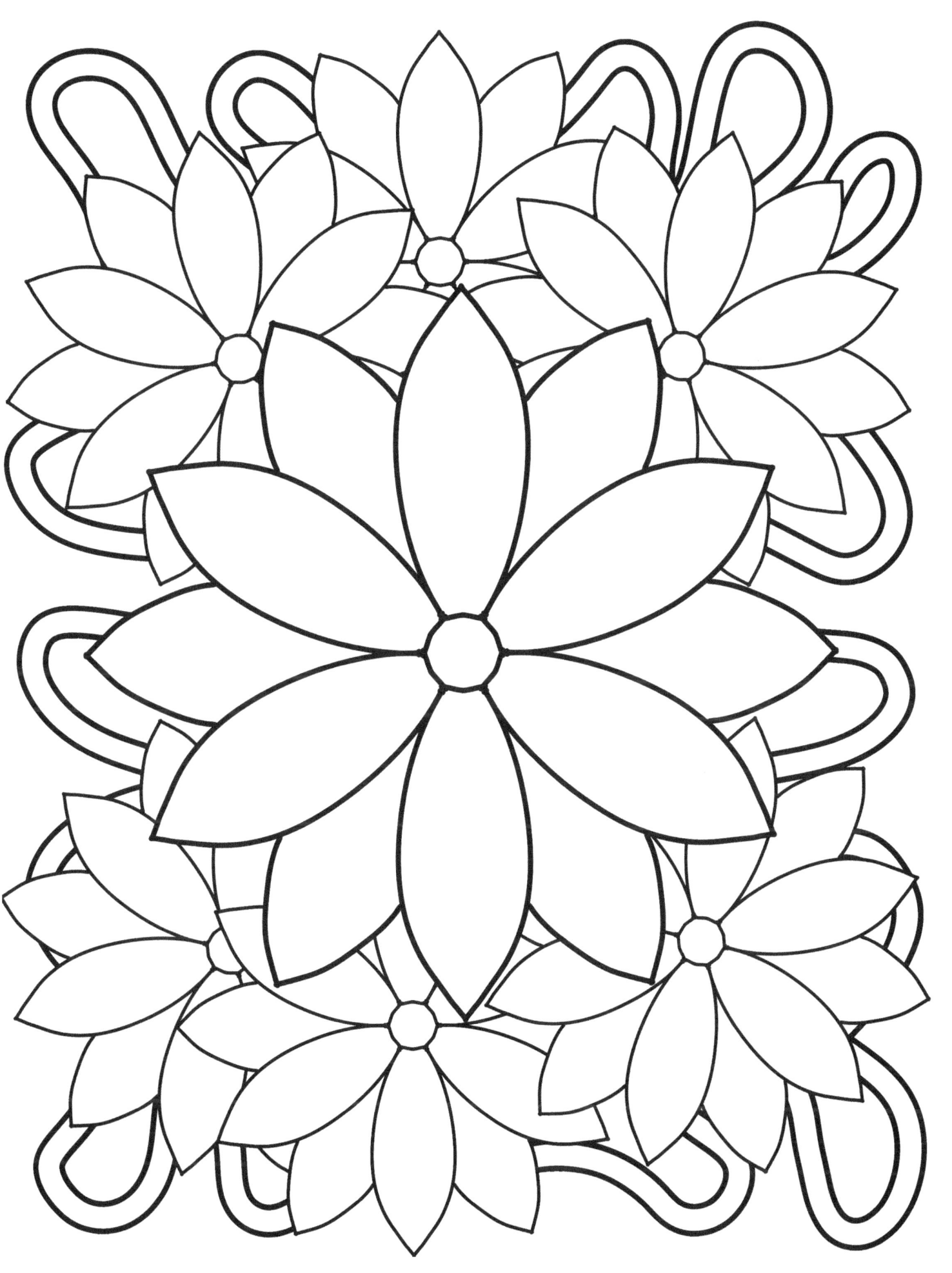

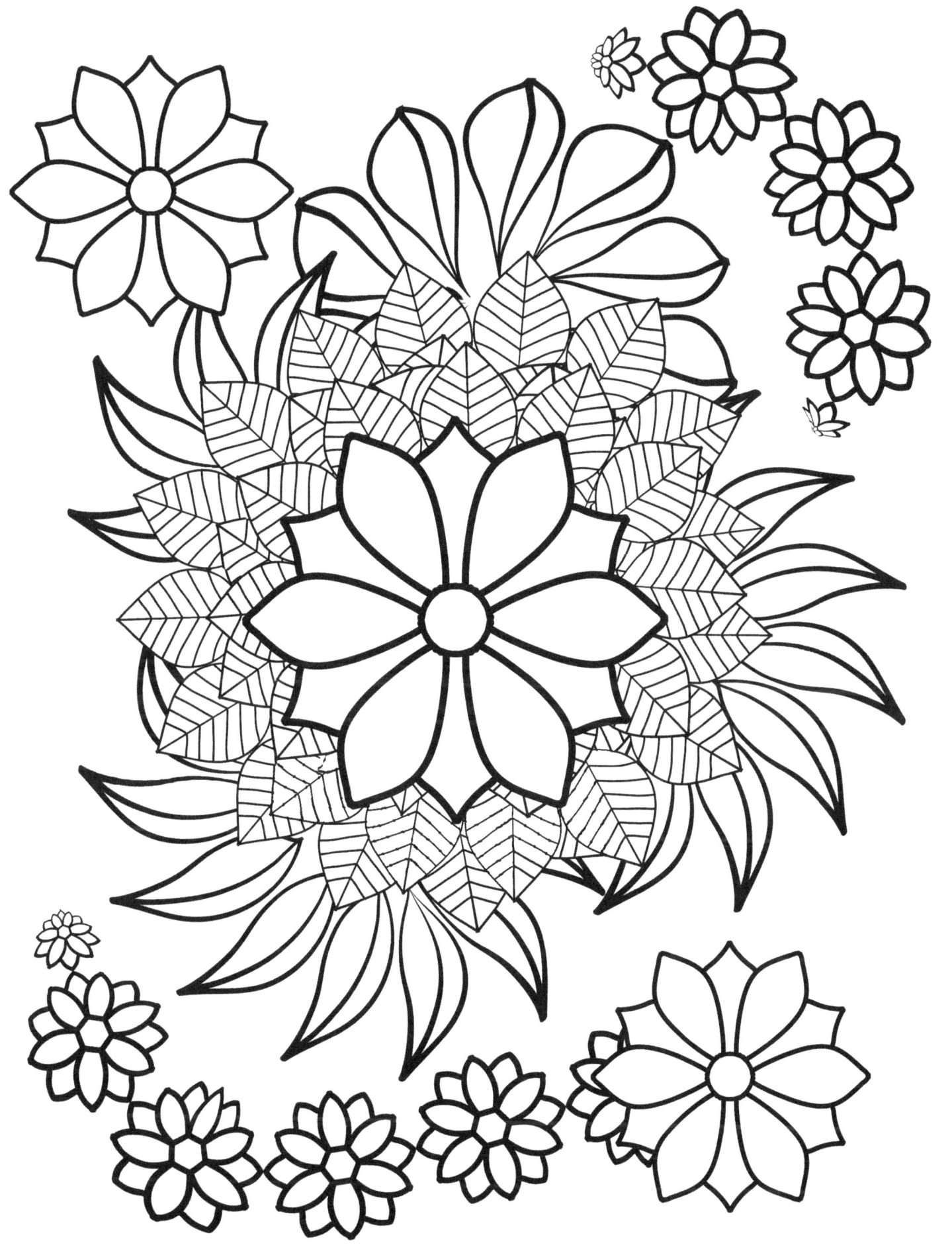

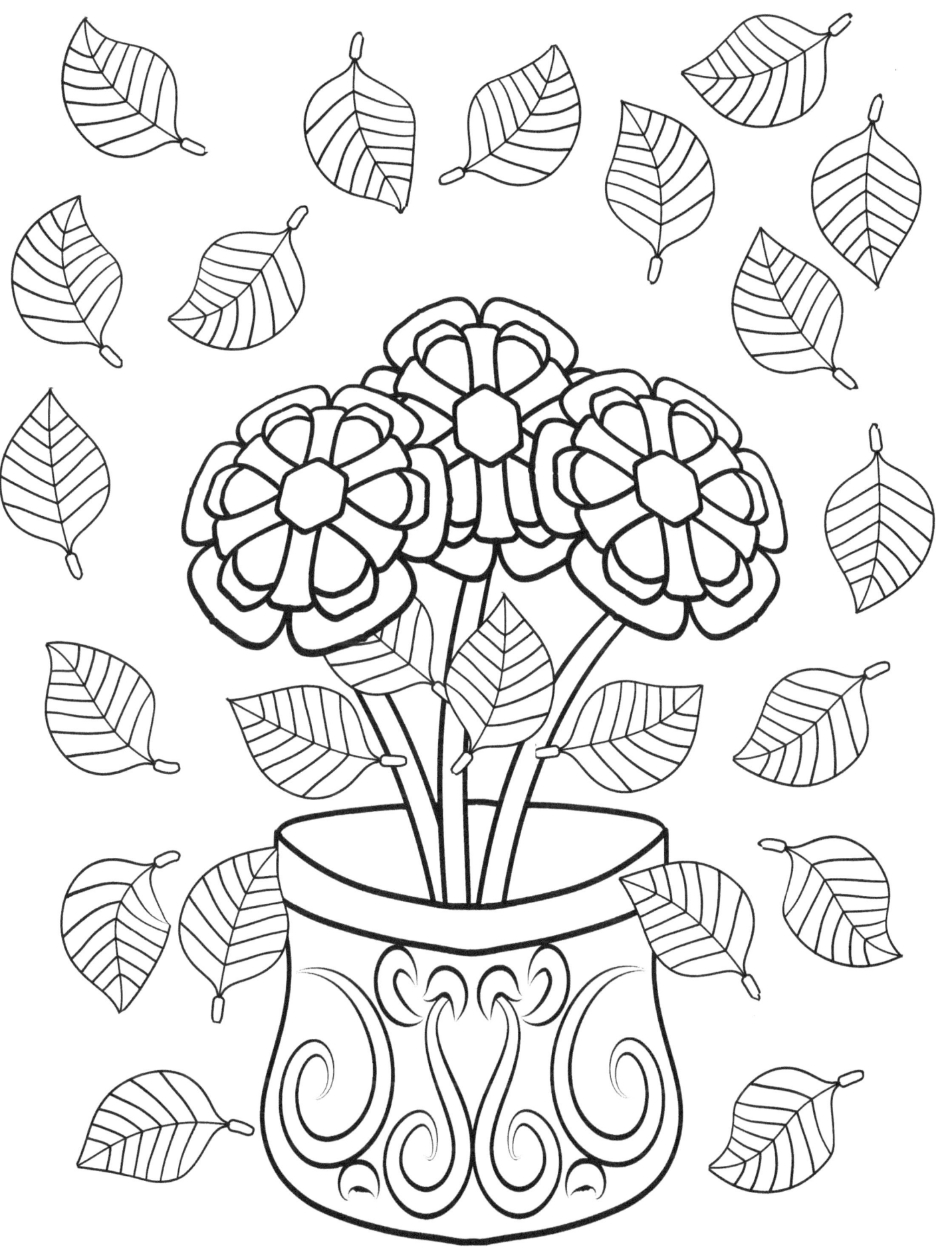

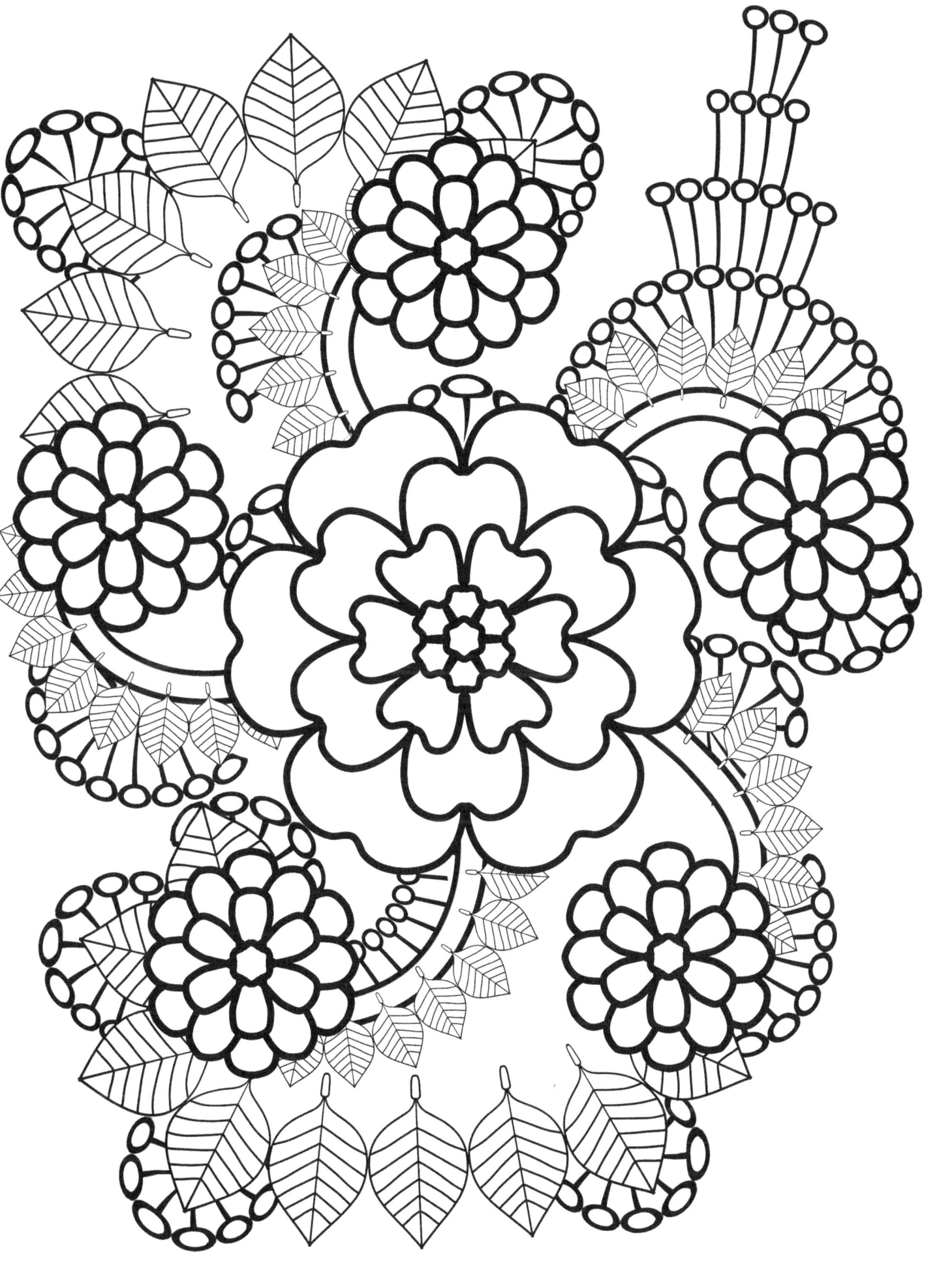

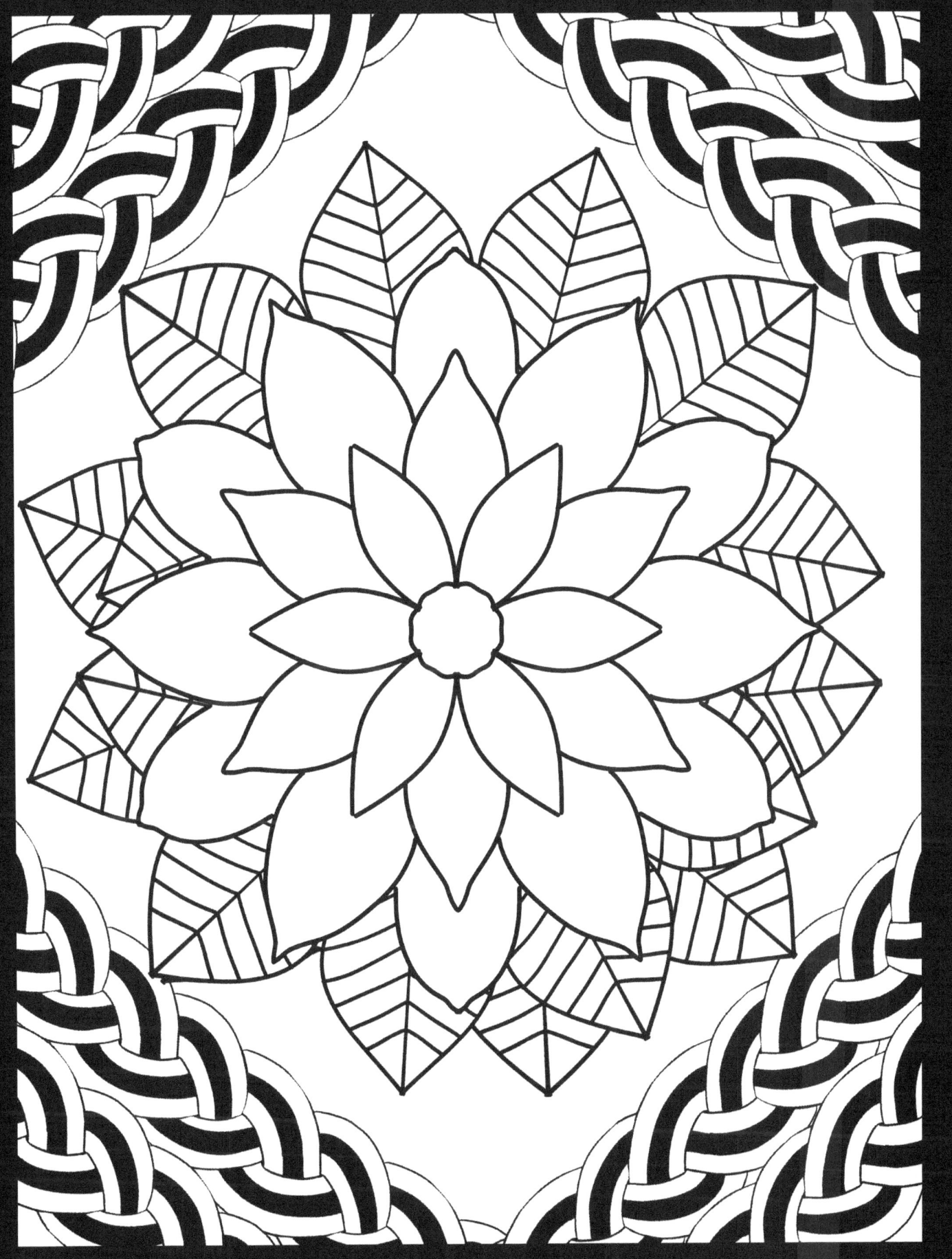

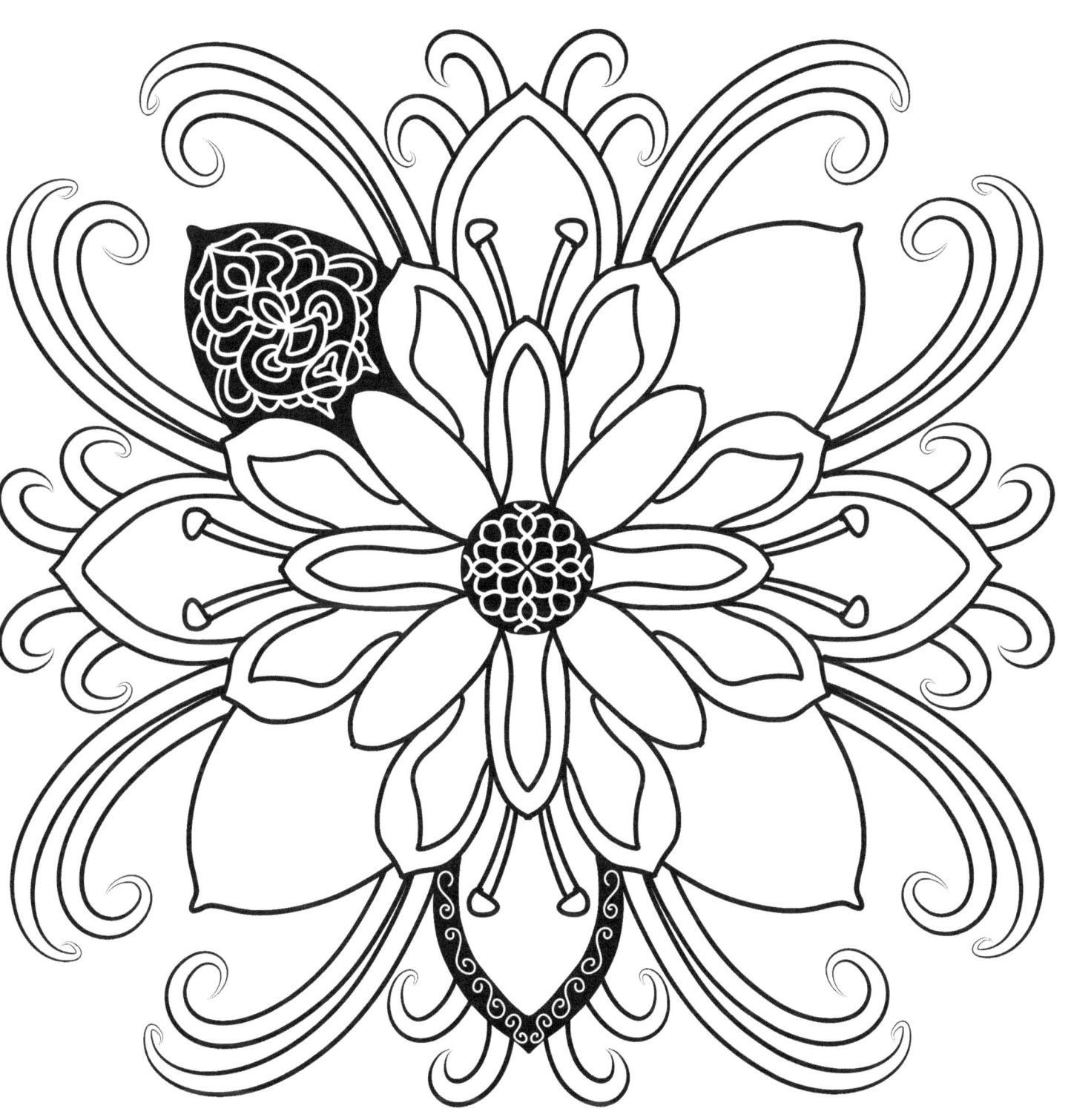

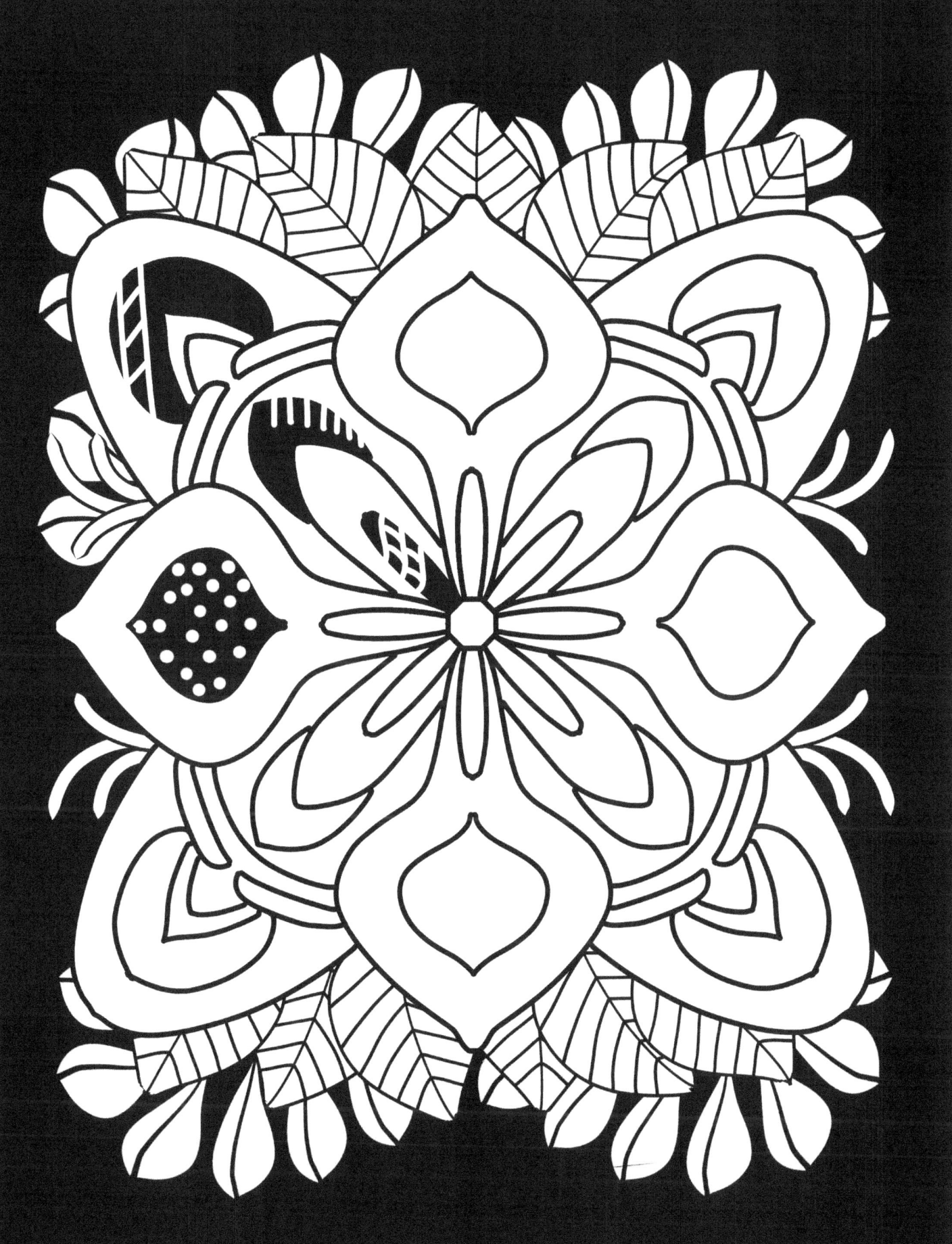

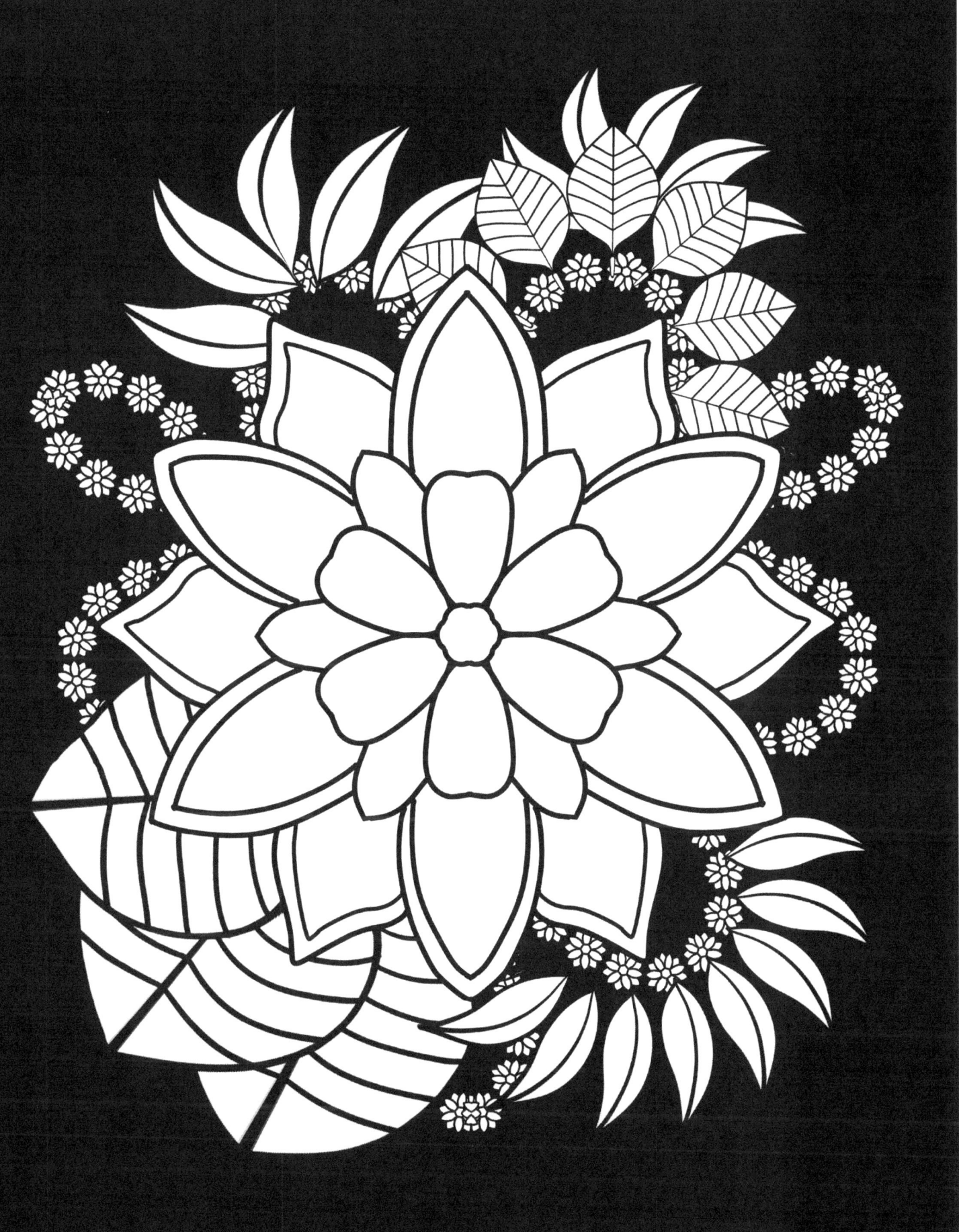

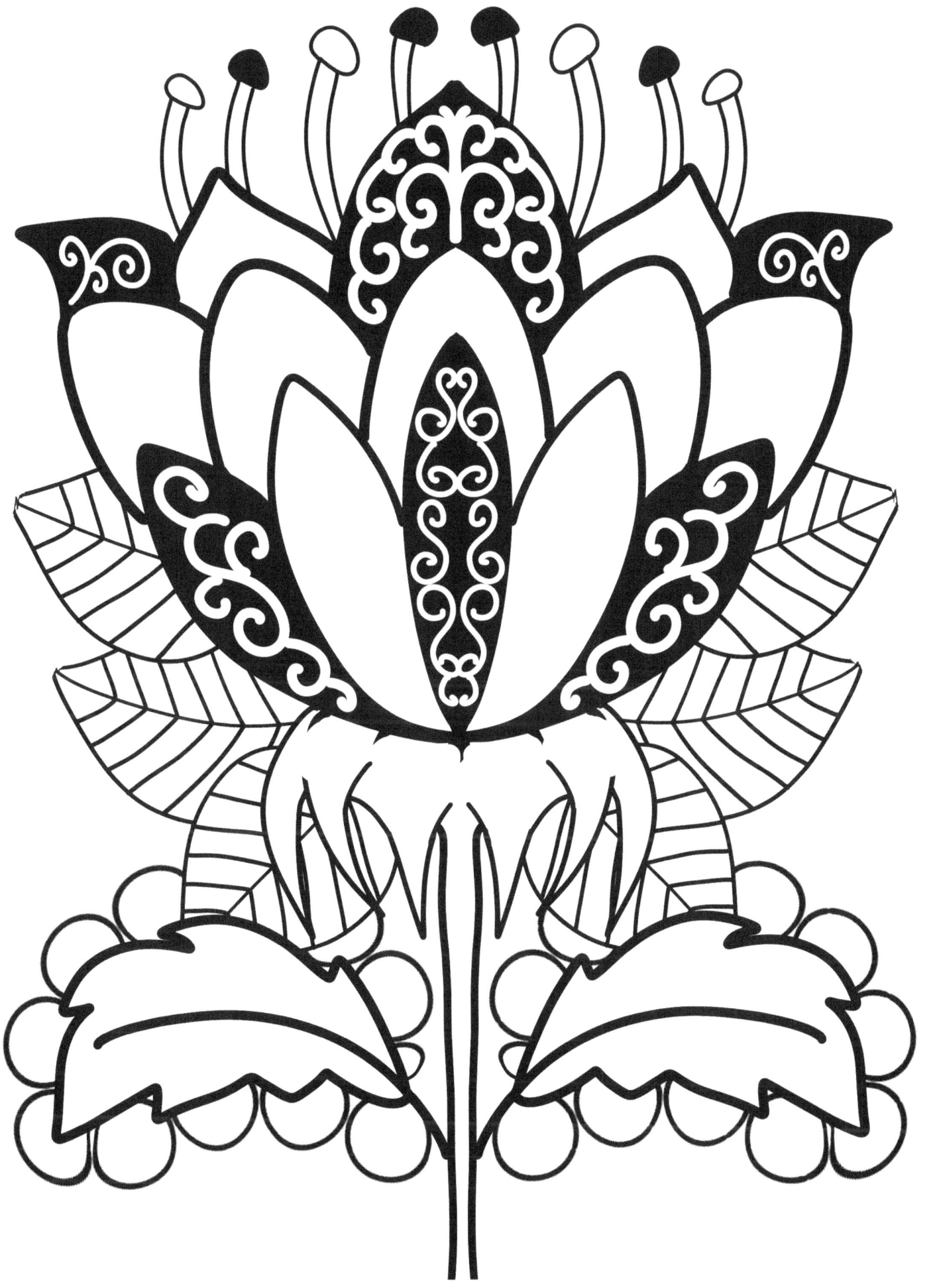

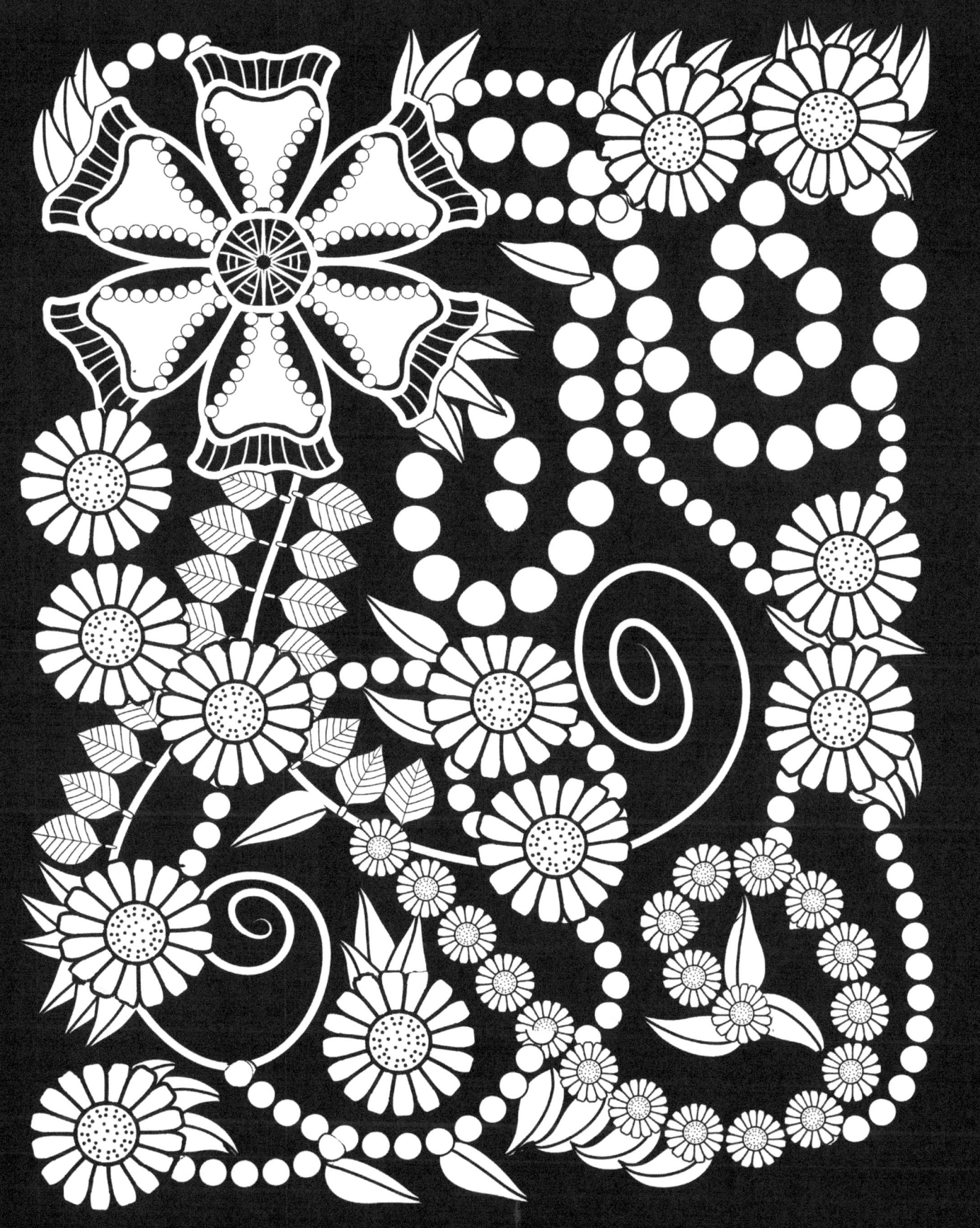

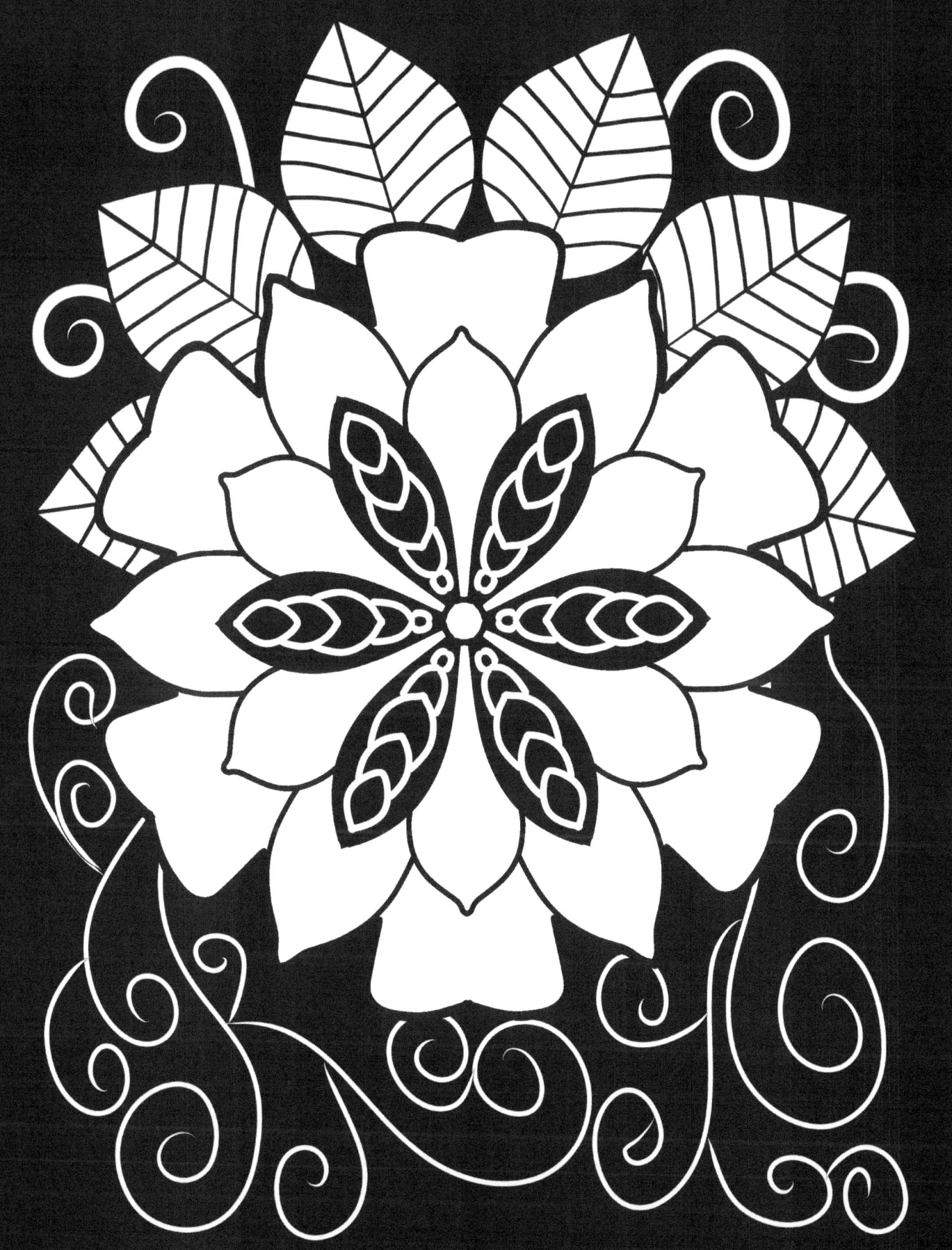

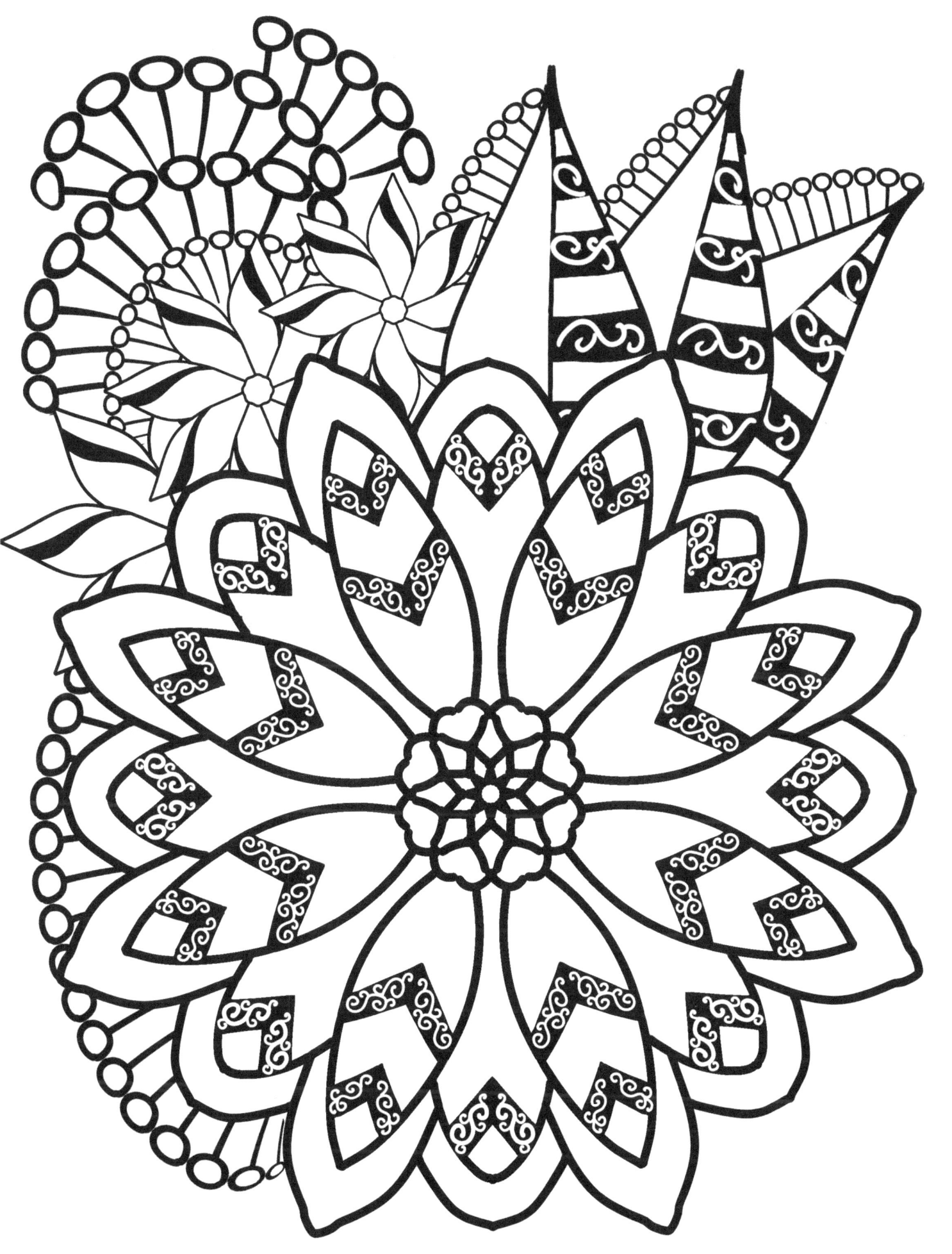

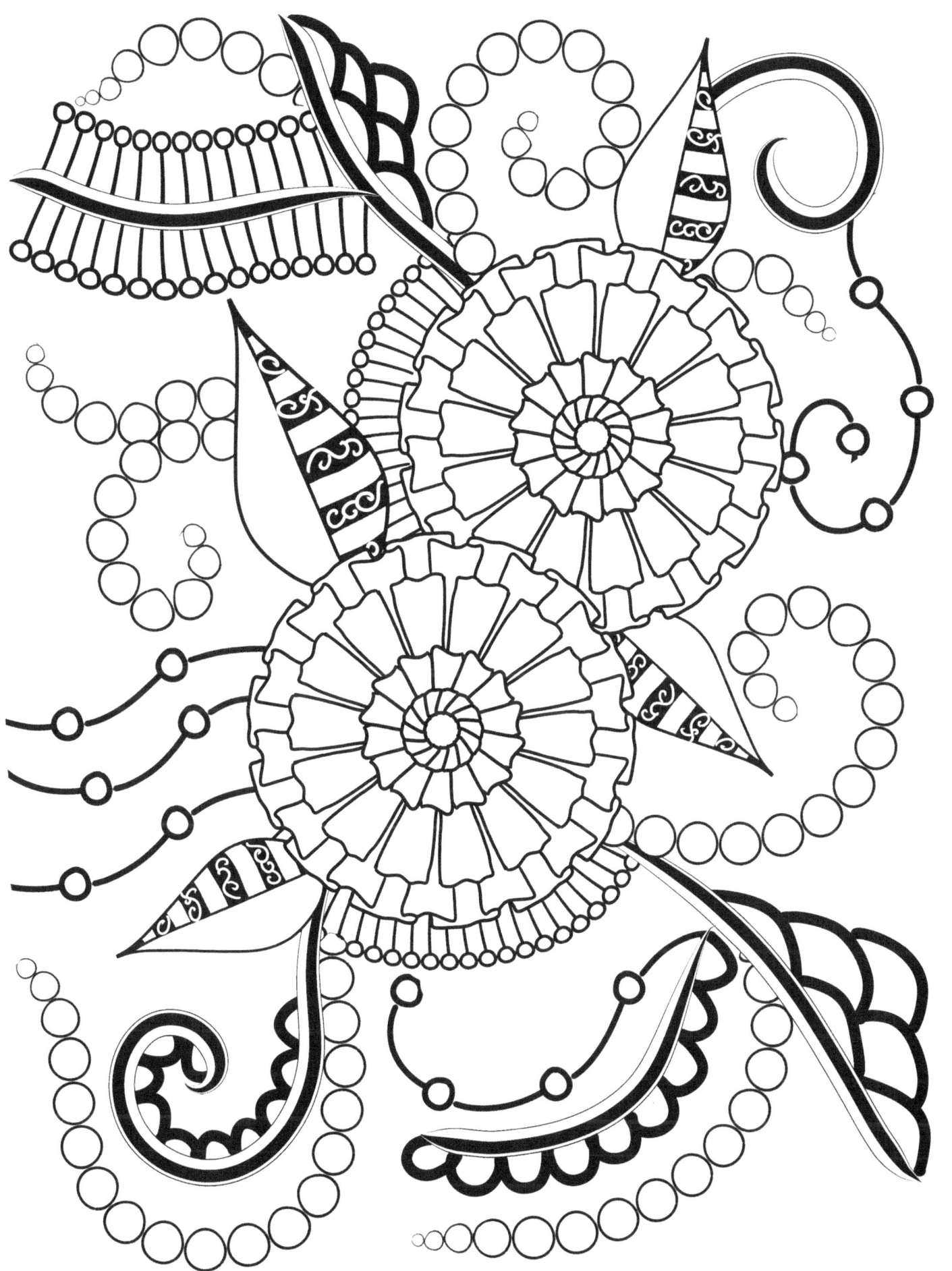

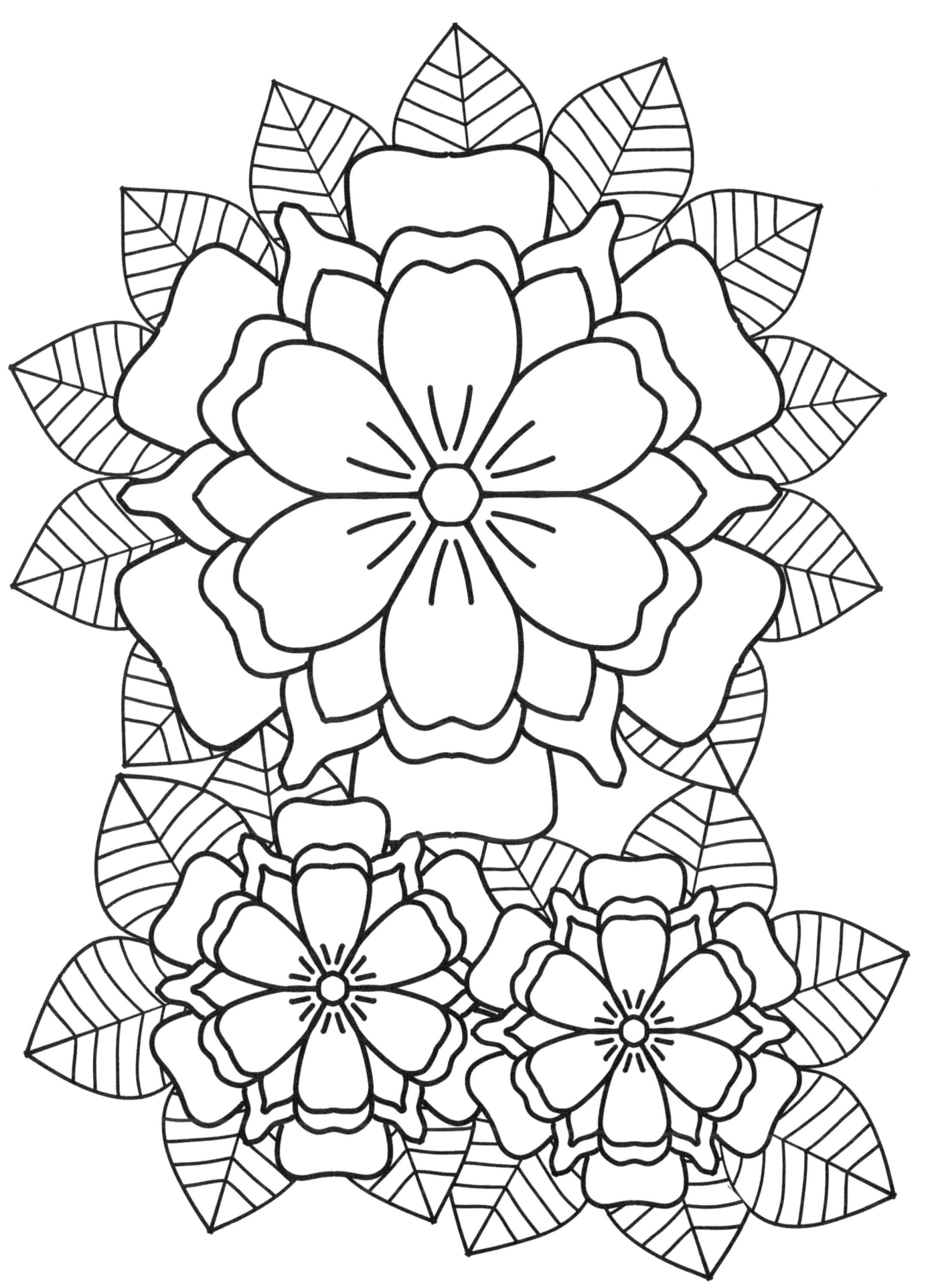

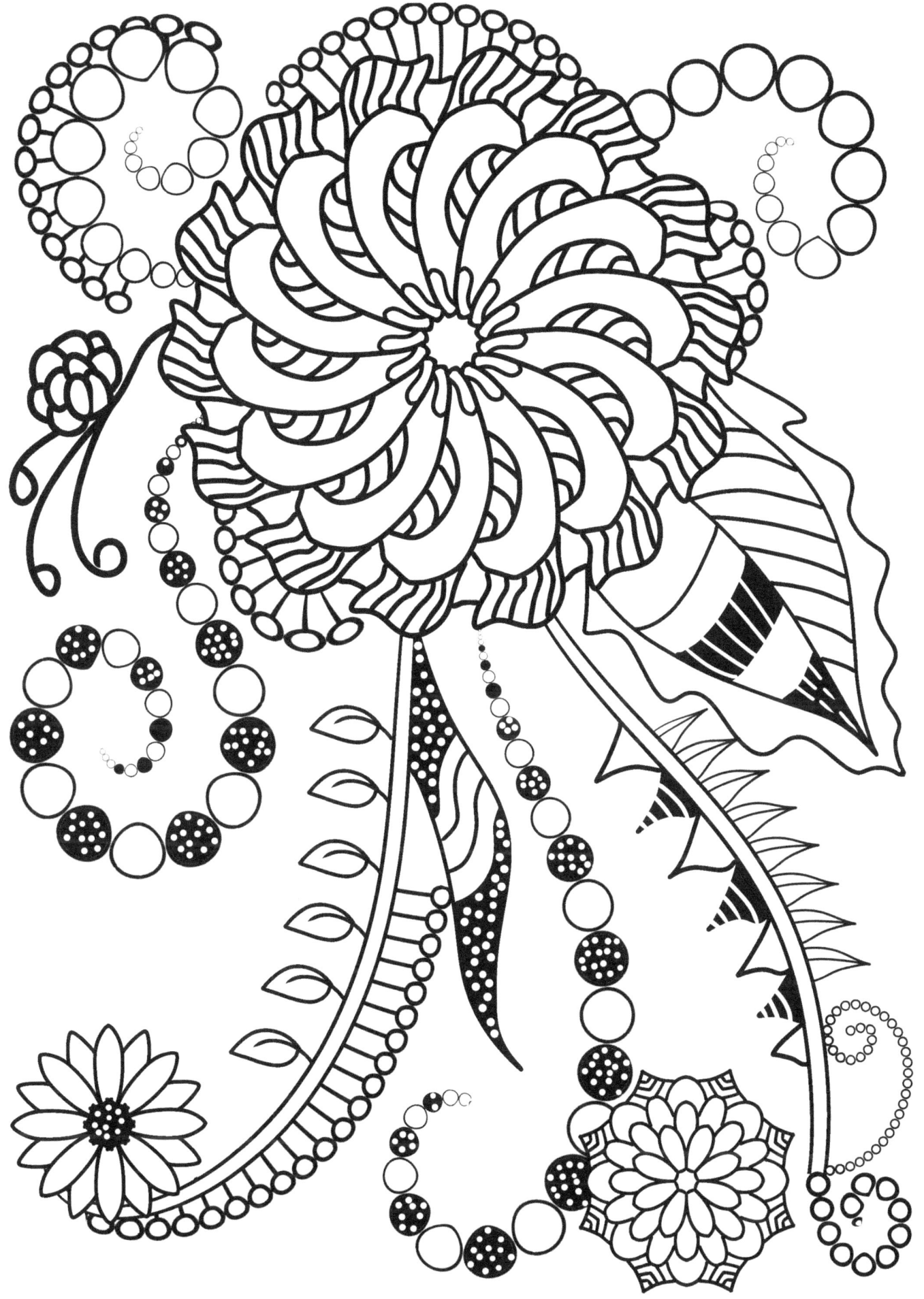

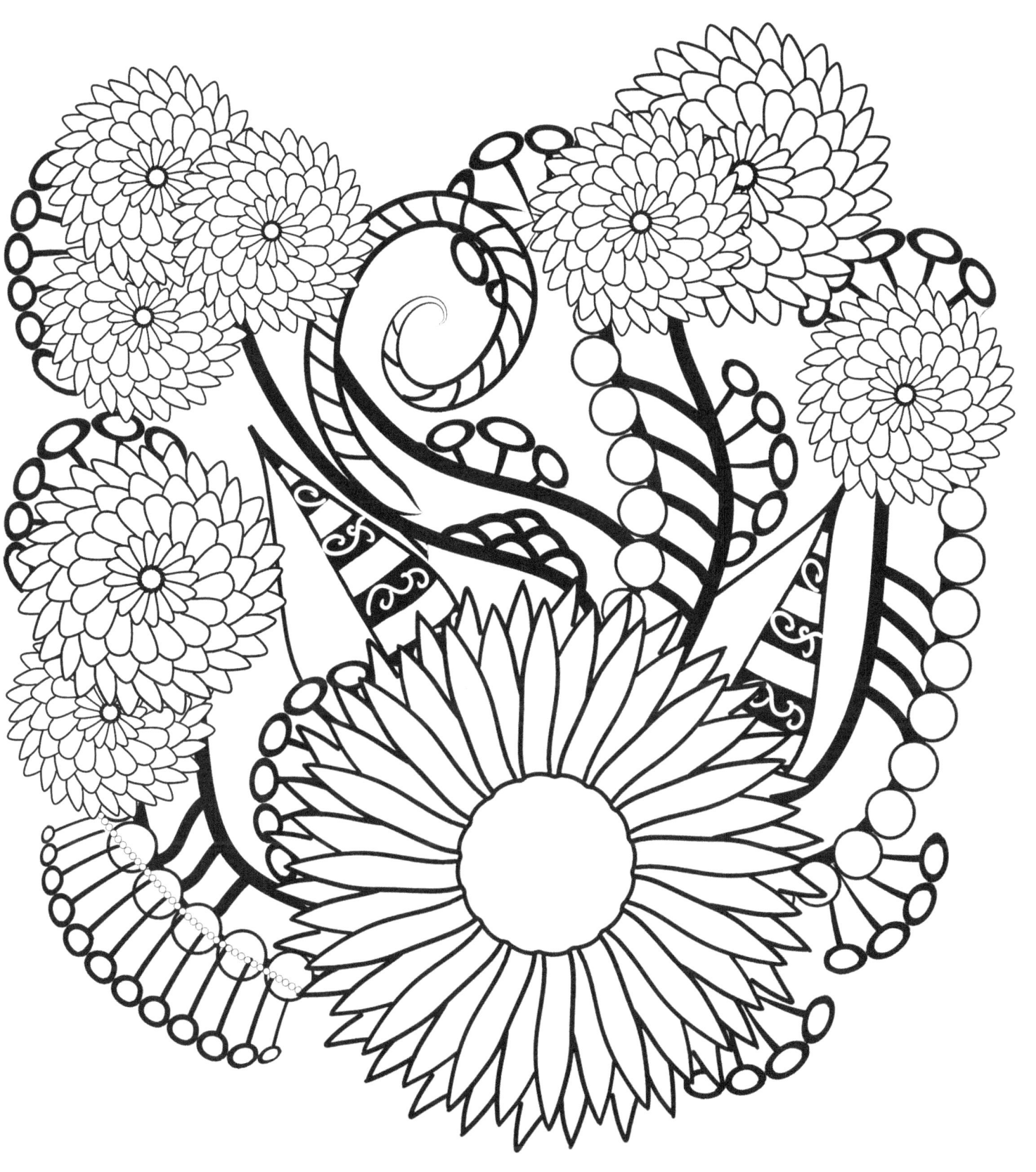

For more designs and upcoming books, please visit our facebook group at :

@coloringbooksandmandalas

http://www.asmazergui.com